Strategic Intervention
Assessment Book

Grades 4-6

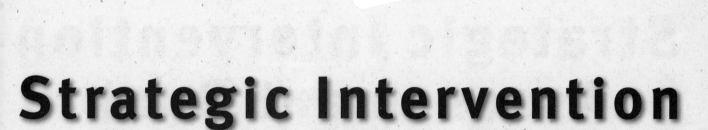

Harcourt School Publishers

www.harcourtschool.com

Strategic Intervention
Assessment Book

Grades 4-6

Harcourt School Publishers

www.harcourtschool.com

Printed in the United States of America

ISBN 10 0-15-365586-0

ISBN 13 978-0-15-365586-9

6 7 8 9 10 170 16 15 14 13 12 11 10 09

Table of Contents

• •

Grade 6

Oral Reading Fluency Assessment

What Is Oral Reading Fluency?

Research recognizes fluency as a strong indicator of efficient and proficient reading. A fluent reader reads orally with accuracy and expression, at a speech-like pace. Oral reading fluency is an assessment of accuracy and rate. It is expressed as the number of words read correctly per minute (WCPM).

Reading researchers have demonstrated the importance of "automaticity," or reading automatically. If a reader devotes most of his or her attention to pronouncing words, comprehension and meaning will suffer. On the other hand, students who read fluently can devote more attention to meaning and thus increase their comprehension. This is why oral reading fluency is an important goal of reading instruction, especially in the elementary grades.

Assessing oral reading fluency helps a teacher —

◆ determine how well a student can apply decoding skills and recognize high frequency words

◆ plan instruction in word analysis and decoding

◆ evaluate the effects of special instruction designed to improve decoding skills

What Passages Will I Use?

The oral reading passages contained in this booklet are designed to provide you with the tools for assessing oral reading fluency from Grades 4 through 6. Six passages are provided for each grade. The "A" passages are intended for the beginning of the school year; the "B" passages are intended for the middle of the school year; and the "C" passages are for the end of the school year.

The passages provide a mixture of narrative text and exposition. All of the passages are original to ensure that students are not familiar with them. The readability of the passages has been controlled so that the difficulty increases from the beginning of the school year through the end of the school year within each grade. The difficulty also increases incrementally from grade to grade.

The table below shows which passage to use for each grade level at various times during the school year.

Grade	Beginning of School Year (first three months)	Middle of School Year (second three months)	End of School Year (last three months)
4	4A1, 4A2	4B1, 4B2	4C1, 4C2
5	5A1, 5A2	5B1, 5B2	5C1, 5C2
6	6A1, 6A2	6B1, 6B2	6C1, 6C2

Although the passages are representative of the text difficulty that students are expected to read at each grade level, at times it may be necessary to "test out of level" and use a lower level passage.

Some teachers may be interested in monitoring a student's oral reading fluency periodically throughout the school year. To do so, use the A passages at the beginning of the year, the B passages at the middle of the year, and the C passages at the end of the year. Record the oral reading fluency scores from multiple administrations on the Record of Progress form located on page 2.

How Do I Assess Oral Reading Fluency?

Assessing oral reading fluency can be done quickly and easily. Have a student read one of the passages orally while you time the reading and record the reading errors on the Oral Reading Fluency Recording Form.

To administer the oral reading fluency assessment you will need the following:

◆ a stopwatch or watch with a second hand
◆ a copy of the passage for the student to read
◆ a copy of the Recording Form for the same passage for you to mark as the student reads

Once you have selected the passage you will use, follow these steps to conduct the assessment:

1. Explain the task to the student. Tell the student that you want to see how well he or she can read aloud. Inform the student that you will follow along as he or she reads, taking notes. The student may ask about the stopwatch and being timed. Encourage the student to read at his or her "normal" pace. You don't want the student to speed up and read artificially fast because of the timing.

2. Have the student begin. Use the stopwatch or second hand to time a one-minute interval as inconspicuously as possible.

3. As the student reads, unobtrusively record reading errors on the Recording Form. Mark mispronunciations, substitutions, omissions of a sound or word, and other errors. *Do not count repetitions, self-corrections, or mispronunciations of proper nouns as reading errors.*

4. When the stopwatch or second hand reaches the one-minute mark, place a slash mark on the Oral Reading Fluency Recording Form after the last word the student reads. Tell the student to stop reading.

How Do I Compute the Fluency Score?

At the bottom of each Recording Form is a section labeled "Fluency Score." Follow these steps to complete that section and to compute a student's fluency score.

1. Count the total number of words the student read in one minute. The row numbers in the right margin will help you quickly determine the total number. Record this number in the first row, "Total Words Read Per Minute."

2. Count the number of reading errors the student made. Remember, *do not count repetitions, self-corrections, or mispronunciations of proper nouns as errors.* Record this number in the second row, "Number of Errors."

3. Subtract the number of reading errors (row 2) from the total number of words read (row 1). Record the answer in the third row, "Number of Words Read Correctly." This is the student's oral reading fluency score.

How Do I Interpret the Fluency Score?

Several studies have been conducted to determine what the "normal" reading fluency rate is at various grade levels. Perhaps the most notable is a study conducted by Hasbruck and Tindal (1992) in which they established fluency norms for Grades 2 through 5. The tables below are based on the results of their study.

You may use the tables below to make a normative interpretation of a student's oral reading fluency score. A normative interpretation means that you compare the student's performance to the performance of other students at that grade level.

Percentiles are a commonly used norm-referenced score. A percentile score simply indicates the percentage of students likely to score below a certain level. For example, if a Words Correct Per Minute score of 82 is at the 50th percentile for Grade 4, it means that approximately 50 percent of fourth graders would have oral reading fluency scores *below* 82 and about 50 percent of fourth graders would have oral reading fluency scores *above* 82.

A helpful way to interpret percentile scores is to think in terms of "quartiles" or quarters. Percentile scores can be grouped into four quarters.

Interpreting Quartiles

Quartile	Percentile	Level of Performance
1st	1st to 25th	Students in this quartile are significantly below average in oral reading fluency.
2nd	26th to 50th	Students in this quartile may range from moderately to slightly below average.
3rd	51st to 75th	Students in this quartile may range from slightly to moderately above average.
4th	76th to 99th	Students in this quartile are significantly above average in oral reading fluency.

The following three tables show the quartile scores for each grade level for the beginning, middle, and end of the year. To interpret a student's oral reading fluency score, follow these steps:

1. Choose the correct table depending upon the time of year that you tested the student. Was it the beginning, middle, or end of year?

2. Locate the appropriate grade level row for the student you tested.

3. Look across the row and find the column that contains the student's WCPM score. At the top of the column is the quartile that the student falls into.

The following example may illustrate how to interpret a student's score. Suppose you tested Rick, a fifth grader, at the beginning of the school year. Rick read 127 words in one minute but made 10 errors so his WCPM score is 117. Locate the norms table for "Beginning of the Year." Find the row for grade 5. Look across the row until you find a column that contains 117. The third column contains the range 106 – 126. The score of 117 falls within that range, so Rick is in the third quartile in oral reading fluency. His oral reading fluency is "moderately better" than most students at his grade level. One may conclude that he is making better-than-normal progress in acquiring and applying decoding skills.

Oral Reading Fluency Norms
Beginning of the Year

Grade	Quartile			
	1st	2nd	3rd	4th
4	71 and below	72 – 99	100 – 125	126 and above
5	76 and below	77 – 105	106 – 126	127 and above
6	99 and below	100 – 125	126 – 150	151 and above

Oral Reading Fluency Norms
Middle of the Year

Grade	Quartile			
	1st	2nd	3rd	4th
4	88 and below	89 – 112	113 – 133	134 and above
5	92 and below	93 – 118	119 – 143	144 and above
6	99 and below	100 – 125	126 – 150	151 and above

Oral Reading Fluency Norms
End of the Year

Grade	Quartile			
	1st	2nd	3rd	4th
4	91 and below	92 – 118	119 – 143	144 and above
5	99 and below	100 – 128	129 – 151	152 and above
6	99 and below	100 – 150	151 – 170	171 and above

What Can I Do to Improve Oral Reading Fluency?

Research suggests several instructional strategies for improving oral reading fluency. This section gives a brief overview of some of these strategies.

Echo Reading

In this strategy, the teacher serves as a model of what good oral reading fluency sounds like. The teacher reads one sentence of text aloud with appropriate intonation and phrasing while the student follows along in the text. Immediately after the teacher finishes, the student tries to imitate this oral-reading model. This process can be repeated until the student can imitate more than one sentence at a time.

Readers' Theater

This method uses a minimum of props or costumes. Divide a story into parts for each character and one or more narrators. Assign parts to individual students. Allow students to practice their parts by reading orally. Stress fluency. The story should be "performed" for an audience (usually other class members).

Choral Reading

Select a poem and read it to a group of students. Practice reading the poem with students until they can read it in "one voice." You may organize the students into groups and assign various parts to each. Have students "perform" the poem for an audience.

Paired Reading

Pair up readers to respond to one another. Explain that they will take turns being readers and being listeners. Show them what they should be listening for by modeling fluent reading and nonfluent reading. For example, show the difference between smooth and choppy reading. Show how expressive readers make their voices go higher and lower, faster and slower, louder and softer. Then have students take turns being the reader and the listener. The reader reads a selection three times. The listener gives a report after the 2nd and 3rd readings. All reports are complimentary. No criticism or advice is allowed. After the third readings, they switch roles and the listener gets an opportunity to practice fluency. You may also wish to have them time each other's reading.

Repeated Readings

Select a passage that is easy for the student to read. Model the passage by reading it aloud to the student. Encourage the student to read it aloud and tape record his reading. Have the student replay the tape and listen to his reading. Another variation is to have him time his reading using a stopwatch and count the errors he makes. Then have the student repeat the process and attempt to increase his rate of reading and decrease the number of errors made. Keeping a personal scorecard can add motivation to this activity.

Neurological Impress Method

Select a short passage that is easy for the student to read. Sit slightly behind the student holding the passage in front of the student so that you speak toward his dominant ear. Read together as in "one voice" as you move along the line of print. The passage should be read slightly beyond the student's normal rate so attention is paid to whole words and sentences.

Appendix: Copying Masters

Oral Reading Fluency

Record of Progress

Name _____ Examiner _____

	Date: _____ Passage: _____	Date: _____ Passage: _____	Date: _____ Passage: _____
Total Words Read per Minute			
Number of Errors			
Words Correct per Minute (WCPM)			
Quartile			
Observations			
Comments			

Oral Reading Passage

Our class assignment was to "build a better mouse house." Robbie and I both entered the cardboard category. We were only allowed to use cardboard and glue to make our mouse houses.

Robbie used the box that his skateboard had come in, and I used a shoebox. We both punched air holes in the tops of our boxes so the mice could breathe, and we both made small doors for our houses. My door opened out and fastened with a cardboard latch, and his door slid up and down.

When the day the assignment was due arrived, I tucked two white mice into my cozy house and took it to school. Robbie did the same, but his mice were gray. Everyone was quiet as Mrs. Hodges walked around the classroom examining one mouse house after another. When she came to mine, she opened the door and out flew those mice. One landed on her foot and another ran under her desk. That's when I found out I was the only person who had brought real mice.

It took the class a half hour to calm down. Of course, I didn't win the contest.

Oral Reading Fluency Recording Form

Name _____ **Date** _____

Passage 4A1   Word Count: 193

Our class assignment was to "build a better mouse	9
house." Robbie and I both entered the cardboard	17
category. We were only allowed to use cardboard and	26
glue to make our mouse houses.	32
Robbie used the box that his skateboard had come	41
in, and I used a shoebox. We both punched air holes in	53
the tops of our boxes so the mice could breathe, and we	65
both made small doors for our houses. My door opened	75
out and fastened with a cardboard latch, and his door	85
slid up and down.	89
When the day the assignment was due arrived, I	98
tucked two white mice into my cozy house and took it	109
to school. Robbie did the same, but his mice were gray.	120
Everyone was quiet as Mrs. Hodges walked around the	129
classroom examining one mouse house after another.	136
When she came to mine, she opened the door and out	147
flew those mice. One landed on her foot and another	157
ran under her desk. That's when I found out I was the	169
only person who had brought real mice.	176
It took the class a half hour to calm down. Of course,	188
I didn't win the contest.	193

© Harcourt

FLUENCY SCORE

Total Words Read Per Minute	_____
Number of Errors —	_____
Number of Words Read Correctly (WCPM)	_____

Oral Reading Passage

Kay's father had been jogging for many years. Every morning before breakfast, Mr. Benson left the house wearing his sneakers and jogging shorts. Lucky, the Bensons' dog, usually ran with him.

Now Kay was ten years old and wanted to start running. Her father told her that if she did all her homework each night, and got to bed on time, she could run with him for part of his route each day. Kay saved her allowance and got some neat running shoes. The first week, Kay was tired in the afternoon in school, but she didn't tell anyone. She didn't want her parents to make her stop running.

After a few weeks, Kay felt wonderful, and looked forward to running with her father each day. It was a special time for them to be together. Kay began to train to run in the town's three-mile race. She felt confident that she would do well, because she enjoyed running and was getting better each day.

Oral Reading Fluency Recording Form

Name _____ Date _____

Passage 4A2   Word Count: 166

Kay's father had been jogging for many years. Every	9
morning before breakfast, Mr. Benson left the house	17
wearing his sneakers and jogging shorts. Lucky, the Bensons'	26
dog, usually ran with him.	31
Now Kay was ten years old and wanted to start running.	42
Her father told her that if she did all her homework each	54
night, and got to bed on time, she could run with him for	67
part of his route each day. Kay saved her allowance and	78
got some neat running shoes. The first week, Kay was tired	89
in the afternoon in school, but she didn't tell anyone. She	100
didn't want her parents to make her stop running.	109
After a few weeks, Kay felt wonderful, and looked forward	119
to running with her father each day. It was a special time for	132
them to be together. Kay began to train to run in the town's	145
three-mile race. She felt confident that she would do well,	156
because she enjoyed running and was getting better each day.	166

FLUENCY SCORE

Total Words Read Per Minute   _____

Number of Errors   – _____

Number of Words Read Correctly (WCPM)   _____

Assessments for Grades 4–6

Oral Reading Passage

The first step in making crayons is to make the color. At the color mill, water is mixed with different chemicals in large wooden tanks to make each color. Each color has its own tank. The colored solution is poured through a filter, and then most of the water is squeezed out. What is left is a moist cake of color.

Next, workers break up these cakes of color and stack them on plastic trays. Then they put the trays into ovens so that the color cakes will dry. Hard, dry lumps of color come out of the ovens. These lumps are put in a machine that grinds them into a fine colored powder. Workers pour the powder into bags and send the bags to the crayon manufacturing plant.

Outside the manufacturing plant are huge tanks of hot liquid wax. This clear, hot wax is pumped through pipes and mixed in large tubs with the colored powder. The colored wax is stirred and then poured into crayon molds. Cold water flows in pipes around the molds to cool the hot, liquid wax and make it hard.

Once the wax has hardened, it is removed from the molds. A paper label is wrapped around each piece and the crayons are packed into boxes.

Oral Reading Fluency Recording Form

Name _____ **Date** _____

Passage 4B1   Word Count: 212

The first step in making crayons is to make the	10
color. At the color mill, water is mixed with different	20
chemicals in large wooden tanks to make each color. Each	30
color has its own tank. The colored solution is poured	40
through a filter, and then most of the water is squeezed	51
out. What is left is a moist cake of color.	61

Next, workers break up these cakes of color and   70
stack them on plastic trays. Then they put the trays into   81
ovens so that the color cakes will dry. Hard, dry lumps of   93
color come out of the ovens. These lumps are put in a   105
machine that grinds them into a fine colored powder.   114
Workers pour the powder into bags and send the bags to   125
the crayon manufacturing plant.   129

Outside the manufacturing plant are huge tanks of   137
hot liquid wax. This clear, hot wax is pumped through   147
pipes and mixed in large tubs with the colored powder.   157
The colored wax is stirred and then poured into crayon   167
molds. Cold water flows in pipes around the molds to cool   178
the hot, liquid wax and make it hard.   186

Once the wax has hardened, it is removed from the   196
molds. A paper label is wrapped around each piece and   206
the crayons are packed into boxes.   212

© Harcourt

FLUENCY SCORE

Total Words Read Per Minute   _____
Number of Errors   −   _____
Number of Words Read Correctly (WCPM)   _____

Oral Reading Passage

Benny walked over to Grandma Cooper's. He often did that when he was feeling down. Besides, no one there would recognize him as the guy who kept the Seventh Avenue Sluggers from winning the pennant for the third summer in a row.

Grandma Cooper sat, thinking about how sad her grandson looked. "So what's going on, Benny?"

Benny started to explain but couldn't. How could she understand the misery he felt after striking out in the top of the ninth inning?

"You know," Grandma Cooper began, "it's only a game." She walked over to a small table to pick up an old album, which she opened and showed Benny. "I guess you're not the only one in the family who's felt a little low after a ball game."

The headline over the article surrounding the picture read, "Redwings Lose 3-2." The caption under the picture said, "Betty Turner, catcher for the Milltown Batters, tags out Florence Baker as the Redwing outfielder tries to steal home."

"I didn't know you played baseball, Grandma!" Benny said.

"Softball," Grandma Cooper said, remembering the unhappy day in that picture. "Women's softball was in fashion and was quite the rage back then. I lost the championship for my teammates and never got the chance to make it up to them. At least you'll have a chance to play again next summer with the Sluggers."

Oral Reading Fluency Recording Form

Name _____   Date _____

Passage 4B2   Word Count: 229

Benny walked over to Grandma Cooper's. He often did that	10
when he was feeling down. Besides, no one there would recognize	21
him as the guy who kept the Seventh Avenue Sluggers from winning	33
the pennant for the third summer in a row.	42
Grandma Cooper sat, thinking about how sad her grandson looked.	52
"So what's going on, Benny?"	57
Benny started to explain but couldn't. How could she understand	67
the misery he felt after striking out in the top of the ninth inning?	81
"You know," Grandma Cooper began, "it's only a game." She	91
walked over to a small table to pick up an old album, which she opened	106
and showed Benny. "I guess you're not the only one in the family who's	120
felt a little low after a ball game."	128
The headline over the article surrounding the picture read,	137
"Redwings Lose 3-2." The caption under the picture said, "Betty Turner,	148
catcher for the Milltown Batters, tags out Florence Baker as the Redwing	160
outfielder tries to steal home."	165
"I didn't know you played baseball, Grandma!" Benny said.	174
"Softball," Grandma Cooper said, remembering the unhappy day	182
in that picture. "Women's softball was in fashion and was quite the rage	195
back then. I lost the championship for my teammates and never got the	208
chance to make it up to them. At least you'll have a chance to play	223
again next summer with the Sluggers."	229

© Harcourt

FLUENCY SCORE

Total Words Read Per Minute   _____

Number of Errors   —   _____

Number of Words Read Correctly (WCPM)   _____

Oral Reading Passage

Lizards and snakes are closely related reptiles, but they have many different traits. Both are cold-blooded, which means that their body temperatures change with their surroundings, forcing them to seek sunlight to get warm and shade to cool off. Both are covered with dry scales. These scales are not as hard as the shell of a turtle, nor as tough as the skin of a crocodile. Their scales are more flexible and allow freer movement than the turtle's shell or the crocodile's skin.

Lizards usually have four legs. Sometimes they have two, or no legs at all. Some lizards that burrow into the ground are legless and have long, thin bodies. Are these legless lizards snakes? No, there are other ways to tell snakes from lizards.

Snakes do not have eyelids, which lizards do. A clear scale that cannot move covers each snake eye. Snakes can only stare. This is why there are so many stories about snake eyes. Ear openings are something else that lizards have and snakes do not. Because of this, snakes cannot hear a sound. A snake's other senses are excellent, however. A snake has a good sense of touch and can feel the smallest vibration. Some people believe the snake uses its tongue as a weapon. In fact, a snake only uses its tongue to taste the ground, in its search for food.

Oral Reading Fluency Recording Form

Name _____ **Date** _____

Passage 4C1   Word Count: 229

Lizards and snakes are closely related reptiles, but they	**9**
have many different traits. Both are cold-blooded, which	**18**
means that their body temperatures change with their surroundings,	**27**
forcing them to seek sunlight to get warm and shade to cool off.	**40**
Both are covered with dry scales. These scales are not as hard	**52**
as the shell of a turtle, nor as tough as the skin of a crocodile.	**67**
Their scales are more flexible and allow freer movement than the	**78**
turtle's shell or the crocodile's skin.	**84**
Lizards usually have four legs. Sometimes they have two, or	**94**
no legs at all. Some lizards which burrow into the ground are	**106**
legless and have long, thin bodies. Are these legless lizards snakes?	**117**
No, there are other ways to tell snakes from lizards.	**127**
Snakes do not have eyelids, which lizards do. A clear scale	**138**
that cannot move covers each snake eye. Snakes can only stare.	**149**
This is why there are so many stories about snake eyes. Ear	**161**
openings are something else which lizards have and snakes do not.	**172**
Because of this, snakes cannot hear a sound. A snake's other	**183**
senses are excellent, however. A snake has a good sense of	**194**
touch and can feel the smallest vibration. Some people believe	**204**
the snake uses its tongue as a weapon. In fact, a snake only uses	**218**
its tongue to taste the ground, in its search for food.	**229**

© Harcourt

FLUENCY SCORE

Total Words Read Per Minute	_____
Number of Errors −	_____
Number of Words Read Correctly (WCPM)	_____

Assessments for Grades 4–6

Oral Reading Passage

You have probably seen people having yard sales. They set up tables in their yard or garage. Then they put price tags on things that they want to sell and place the items on the tables for shoppers to look at. Yard sales are a great way to clean clutter out of the house.

To have a yard sale, all you need is a collection of items that are in good condition but are no longer useful to you. Price each item for a lot less than it would cost if it were new. If you don't have enough things to sell, invite a friend or neighbor to join you for a combined sale.

You can make it easier for shoppers to find something to buy by organizing your sale items. For example, put all books together in one area, and toys in another area.

You should probably make some signs to let people in the neighborhood know about the sale. As the sale goes on, you can lower the prices on things that are not selling. If your sale goes well, you may have a handful of cash at the end of the day!

Oral Reading Fluency Recording Form

Name _____ Date _____

Passage 4C2   Word Count: 195

You have probably seen people having yard sales.	8
They set up tables in their yard or garage. Then they put	20
price tags on things that they want to sell and place the	32
items on the tables for shoppers to look at. Yard sales are a	45
great way to clean clutter out of the house.	54
To have a yard sale, all you need is a collection of	66
items that are in good condition but are no longer useful	77
to you. Price each item for a lot less than it would cost if it	92
were new. If you don't have enough things to sell, invite a	104
friend or neighbor to join you for a combined sale.	114
You can make it easier for shoppers to find	123
something to buy by organizing your sale items. For	132
example, put all books together in one area, and toys in	143
another area.	145
You should probably make some signs to let people	154
in the neighborhood know about the sale. As the sale goes	165
on, you can lower the prices on things that are not selling.	177
If your sale goes well, you may have a handful of cash at	190
the end of the day!	195

© Harcourt

FLUENCY SCORE

Total Words Read Per Minute   _____
Number of Errors   −   _____
Number of Words Read Correctly (WCPM)   _____

Oral Reading Passage

Robert floated contentedly on his back and let the gentle ocean waves push him toward the shore, just a few yards away. The sky was a perfect blue, and the afternoon sun warmed the swimmers as they splashed in the surf. Soon it would be time for Robert and his sister Anna to go home, but for now if felt good to relax in the water.

Suddenly Robert heard a shout. "Help, please help! Somebody help her!" a woman's voice called in panic.

"She's drowning!" someone else yelled frantically.

Robert's toes touched the sand, and he stood up as he heard Anna's urgent voice. "She's over there, Robert! Get her!" Anna seemed to be pointing to the waves near Robert. Looking around quickly, he saw something bobbing just under the surface of the water close by.

Without taking time to answer, Robert dove and reached for the child. His fingers closed around a tiny arm. Grasping the child with strong hands, Robert lifted her out of the water. She coughed and then began to cry. With relief, Robert realized that her loud wail meant that she would be all right.

Oral Reading Fluency Recording Form

Name _____ Date _____

Passage 5A1   Word Count: 190

Robert floated contentedly on his back and let the gentle	10
ocean waves push him toward the shore, just a few yards away.	22
The sky was a perfect blue, and the afternoon sun warmed the	34
swimmers as they splashed in the surf. Soon it would be time for	47
Robert and his sister Anna to go home, but for now if felt good to	62
relax in the water.	66
Suddenly Robert heard a shout. "Help, please help!	74
Somebody help her!" a woman's voice called in panic.	83
"She's drowning!" someone else yelled frantically.	89
Robert's toes touched the sand, and he stood up as he heard	101
Anna's urgent voice. "She's over there, Robert! Get her!" Anna	111
seemed to be pointing to the waves near Robert. Looking around	122
quickly, he saw something bobbing just under the surface of the	133
water close by.	136
Without taking time to answer, Robert dove and reached for	146
the child. His fingers closed around a tiny arm. Grasping the	157
child with strong hands, Robert lifted her out of the water. She	169
coughed and then began to cry. With relief, Robert realized that	180
her loud wail meant that she would be all right.	190

FLUENCY SCORE

Total Words Read Per Minute   _____

Number of Errors   − _____

Number of Words Read Correctly (WCPM) _____

Assessments for Grades 4–6

Oral Reading Passage

Kate stepped out of the plane into a burst of dry desert heat. Though it was October, it felt as if she was walking straight into an oven. Across the runway, the terminal where her father waited shimmered in the heat waves. "I can't believe I was looking forward to warm winters!" she thought with a frown. "After two months of this I'll be missing New York's December slush!"

Her mother nudged her in the back and said, "Dad's waving, Katy." Kate forgot the heat as she waved back. Dad looked tan and happy. Maybe in a few weeks she'd look that happy, too. Maybe she'd forget this lonely feeling. Before Kate knew it, she was running into her father's arms. "We missed you, Dad!" She willed herself not to cry. Stop it, Kate, she told herself. You're not a kid anymore—you're practically a teenager!

After a short drive, Kate got out of the car to find herself in front of a one-story house surrounded by cactus. The air had a freshness to it, she noticed. Suddenly a huge bird popped its head out of a hole in one of the cactus plants, and Kate laughed in surprise.

"Come around back," said her dad. "There's something I want to show you." More cactus, I bet, thought Kate as she trudged along behind him and thought about her friends back home.

Kate stepped around to the back of the house, and there it was! A great amber-colored horse stood watching her with curiosity from a corral. "Dad! " It was all she could say. Kate threw her arms around her father and hugged him hard.

Oral Reading Fluency Recording Form

Name _____ Date _____

Passage 5A2   Word Count: 276

Kate stepped out of the plane into a burst of dry desert	12
heat. Though it was October, it felt as if she was walking straight	25
into an oven. Across the runway, the terminal where her father	36
waited shimmered in the heat waves. "I can't believe I was looking	48
forward to warm winters!" she thought with a frown. "After two	59
months of this I'll be missing New York's December slush!"	69
Her mother nudged her in the back and said, "Dad's waving,	80
Katy." Kate forgot the heat as she waved back. Dad looked tan and	93
happy. Maybe in a few weeks she'd look that happy, too. Maybe	105
she'd forget this lonely feeling. Before Kate knew it, she was	116
running into her father's arms. "We missed you, Dad!" She willed	127
herself not to cry. Stop it, Kate, she told herself. You're not a kid	141
anymore—you're practically a teenager!	146
After a short drive, Kate got out of the car to find herself in	160
front of a one-story house surrounded by cactus. The air had a	173
freshness to it, she noticed. Suddenly a huge bird popped its head	185
out of a hole in one of the cactus plants, and Kate laughed in	199
surprise.	200
"Come around back," said her dad. "There's something I	209
want to show you." More cactus, I bet, thought Kate as she	221
trudged along behind him and thought about her friends back home.	232
Kate stepped around to the back of the house, and there it	244
was! A great amber-colored horse stood watching her with	254
curiosity from a corral. "Dad! " It was all she could say. Kate	266
threw her arms around her father and hugged him hard.	276

© Harcourt

FLUENCY SCORE

Total Words Read Per Minute   _____

Number of Errors   − _____

Number of Words Read Correctly (WCPM) _____

Assessments for Grades 4–6

Oral Reading Passage

Jenny was excited when she finally became a member of the baseball team. Most of the team hadn't wanted a girl to join, but her cousin Roger had convinced them she would help win games. Roger knew she was a better pitcher than any of the other team members.

Tonight, after six innings, the team was behind. Jenny watched nervously, knowing this might be her chance to pitch. Roger urged the coach to send Jenny in. "What will they think if we send a girl out to pitch?" Jenny heard one player say. Suddenly she wasn't nervous; she was angry. She stood up and said, "What will they think if I strike them out?"

"Yeah, give her a try," another player said. Curiosity was rising. The boys wanted to see what she would do.

When Jenny walked up to the pitcher's mound, there were gasps and then jeers from the other team. When she threw her own special pitch, there was silence. When Jenny struck out the third player, her teammates cheered as she walked back to the dugout.

Oral Reading Fluency Recording Form

Name _____ Date _____

Passage 5B1   Word Count: 179

Jenny was excited when she finally became a	8
member of the baseball team. Most of the team hadn't	18
wanted a girl to join, but her cousin Roger had convinced	29
them she would help win games. Roger knew she was a	40
better pitcher than any of the other team members.	49
Tonight, after six innings, the team was behind.	57
Jenny watched nervously, knowing this might be her	65
chance to pitch. Roger urged the coach to send Jenny in.	76
"What will they think if we send a girl out to pitch?"	88
Jenny heard one player say. Suddenly she wasn't nervous;	97
she was angry. She stood up and said, "What will they	108
think if I strike them out?"	114
"Yeah, give her a try," another player said. Curiosity	123
was rising. The boys wanted to see what she would do.	134
When Jenny walked up to the pitcher's mound,	142
there were gasps and then jeers from the other team.	152
When she threw her own special pitch, there was silence.	162
When Jenny struck out the third player, her teammates	171
cheered as she walked back to the dugout.	179

© Harcourt

FLUENCY SCORE

Total Words Read Per Minute   _____
Number of Errors   −   _____
Number of Words Read Correctly (WCPM)   _____

Oral Reading Passage

As soon as it can fly, the monarch butterfly is on the move. It will never walk, since its spindly legs are not strong enough. Its wings can take it wherever it needs to go.

Just as many birds do, monarchs migrate. That is, they move from one region to another as the seasons change. In the autumn, North American monarchs fly south to Mexico. They do not fly alone, but in large flocks. When the monarchs stop to rest, they sometimes cover a whole tree! When they reach their destination in Mexico, the monarchs spend the winter eating.

As spring approaches, the monarchs move back to the north. This time they fly alone. During the trip, the females lay their eggs. The butterflies will die before they reach the place where they started their journey the year before. Their eggs will hatch, and a new generation of monarchs will begin.

Oral Reading Fluency Recording Form

Name _____ Date _____

Passage 5B2   Word Count: 151

As soon as it can fly, the monarch butterfly is on the move.   13

It will never walk, since its spindly legs are not strong enough.   25

Its wings can take it wherever it needs to go.   35

Just as many birds do, monarchs migrate. That is, they   45

move from one region to another as the seasons change. In   56

the autumn, North American monarchs fly south to Mexico.   65

They do not fly alone, but in large flocks. When the monarchs   77

stop to rest, they sometimes cover a whole tree! When they   88

reach their destination in Mexico, the monarchs spend the   97

winter eating.   99

As spring approaches, the monarchs move back to the   108

north. This time they fly alone. During the trip, the females   119

lay their eggs. The butterflies will die before they reach the   130

place where they started their journey the year before. Their   140

eggs will hatch, and a new generation of monarchs will begin.   151

© Harcourt

FLUENCY SCORE

Total Words Read Per Minute   _____

Number of Errors   — _____

Number of Words Read Correctly (WCPM) _____

Oral Reading Passage

Milk is the most nourishing food in the world, and some people say it's the best drink for quenching thirst. Milk has almost all the nutrients we need to grow and to be strong and healthy. All mammals produce milk, but people from the United States, Canada, and other countries think first of the milk that comes from cows. Goat milk is used in Europe, however, and camels provide milk for people who live in northern Africa and the deserts of the Middle East. Some people in South America drink milk from llamas. Reindeer milk is consumed by people who live in Arctic regions. All kinds of milk taste delicious.

One of the reasons cows' milk is so good for you is that 87 percent of it is water. The other 13 percent contains nutrients needed for growth and energy. Milk is such an important food that it is the first food given to newborn babies. A child who drinks milk will grow faster than a child who does not drink any milk. For taste and nutrition, there's nothing better than a tall glass of cold milk.

Oral Reading Fluency Recording Form

Name _____ Date _____

Passage 5C1   Word Count: 187

Milk is the most nourishing food in the world, and some	11
people say it's the best drink for quenching thirst. Milk has	22
almost all the nutrients we need to grow and to be strong and	35
healthy. All mammals produce milk, but people from the United	45
States, Canada, and other countries think first of the milk that	56
comes from cows. Goat milk is used in Europe, however, and	67
camels provide milk for people who live in northern Africa and	78
the deserts of the Middle East. Some people in South America	89
drink milk from llamas. Reindeer milk is consumed by people	99
who live in Arctic regions. All kinds of milk taste delicious.	110
One of the reasons cows' milk is so good for you is that	123
87 percent of it is water. The other 13 percent contains	134
nutrients needed for growth and energy. Milk is such an	144
important food that it is the first food given to newborn babies.	156
A child who drinks milk will grow faster than a child who	168
does not drink any milk. For taste and nutrition, there's	178
nothing better than a tall glass of cold milk.	187

FLUENCY SCORE

Total Words Read Per Minute _____

Number of Errors − _____

Number of Words Read Correctly (WCPM) _____

Oral Reading Passage

Many people assume that tornadoes and hurricanes are the same kind of storm, but they are not. Like all storms, hurricanes and tornadoes are marked by disruptions in the atmosphere such as wind, rain, snow, and hail. However, hurricanes and tornadoes are very different with regard to speed, size, location, and strength.

Tornadoes, which are the most violent storms, happen suddenly. They can pass over a town in several minutes. Hurricanes are much larger and slower than tornadoes. They can take hours or even days to pass over a town. Because of their great size and slow speed, it is much easier to predict the path of hurricanes. The small size and sudden, short life of tornadoes make it difficult to predict their behavior or location.

Hurricanes are frequently 2,000 times larger than an average tornado. However, tornadoes can do twice as much damage, because the average tornado has a wind velocity of 300 miles per hour. Hurricane winds can uproot trees and destroy buildings. Houses, cows, cars, and even trains can be carried up into the atmosphere in tornado winds. In some cases, tornadoes can spring up within a hurricane. The combined effect of these two violent storms can be truly devastating.

Both kinds of storms happen all over the world. Tornadoes occur in England, Asia, Africa, Australia, and the United States. In the United States, tornadoes are most common in the central plains. Sometimes tornadoes happen over water. Hurricanes also occur in many different countries. The South Atlantic Ocean is the only ocean where hurricanes are unknown. Most hurricanes lose their power when they move further away from the ocean.

© Harcourt

Oral Reading Fluency Recording Form

Name _____ Date _____

Passage 5C2   Word Count: 272

Many people assume that tornadoes and hurricanes are the same	10
kind of storm, but they are not. Like all storms, hurricanes and	22
tornadoes are marked by disruptions in the atmosphere such as wind,	33
rain, snow, and hail. However, hurricanes and tornadoes are very	43
different with regard to speed, size, location, and strength.	52

      Tornadoes, which are the most violent storms, happen suddenly.   **61**
They can pass over a town in several minutes. Hurricanes are much   **73**
larger and slower than tornadoes. They can take hours or even days to   **86**
pass over a town. Because of their great size and slow speed, it is much   **101**
easier to predict the path of hurricanes. The small size and sudden,   **113**
short life of tornadoes make it difficult to predict their behavior or   **125**
location.   **126**

      Hurricanes are frequently 2,000 times larger than an average tornado. **136**
However, tornadoes can do twice as much damage, because the   **146**
average tornado has a wind velocity of 300 miles per hour. Hurricane   **158**
winds can uproot trees and destroy buildings. Houses, cows, cars, and   **169**
even trains can be carried up into the atmosphere in tornado winds. In some **183**
cases, tornadoes can spring up within a hurricane. The combined effect   **194**
of these two violent storms can be truly devastating.   **203**

      Both kinds of storms happen all over the world. Tornadoes occur in   **215**
England, Asia, Africa, Australia, and the United States. In the United States, **227**
tornadoes are most common in the central plains. Sometimes   **236**
tornadoes happen over water. Hurricanes also occur in many different   **246**
countries. The South Atlantic Ocean is the only ocean where hurricanes   **257**
are unknown. Most hurricanes lose their power when they move   **267**
further away from the ocean.   **272**

© Harcourt

FLUENCY SCORE

Total Words Read Per Minute   _____
Number of Errors   — _____
Number of Words Read Correctly (WCPM) _____

Assessments for Grades 4–6

Oral Reading Passage

The fans cheered when Central's basketball team won its fifth game in a row. Shawn and Billy, who scored more points than anyone else in the game, wanted to celebrate their victory by going out with their friends. It was very late, though, so Shawn's father suggested that everyone come to their house to celebrate.

"You can order some pizza," Shawn's father said, "if it's all right with everyone's parents."

"That's a wonderful idea," Billy replied. "Thank you, Mr. Potter!"

While Shawn's father went to get his minivan, the other team members asked their parents for permission to go to the pizza party. Billy, Krista, and Jordan, who all lived nearby, got a ride with Mr. Potter. Some of the other players, who lived further away, planned to come with their parents.

On the way home, Mr. Potter stopped and picked up two pizzas. Nick and Rick arrived at Shawn's house with their father, who was carrying two extra-large pizzas. Soon afterward, the car pool from Jefferson Street arrived. Alex, Manny, and Nicole each carried a large, flat box in their hands. The aroma was unmistakable— pepperoni pizza.

"What's happening here?" Shawn's father asked, amazed at the stack of pizzas piling up.

Billy, Shawn, and their friends couldn't believe three sets of pizzas had been ordered. "We could never eat this much pizza," they laughed.

© Harcourt

Oral Reading Fluency Recording Form

Name _____ Date _____

Passage 6A1   Word Count: 226

The fans cheered when Central's basketball team won its fifth	10
game in a row. Shawn and Billy, who scored more points than	22
anyone else in the game, wanted to celebrate their victory by going	34
out with their friends. It was very late, though, so Shawn's father	46
suggested that everyone come to their house to celebrate.	55
"You can order some pizza," Shawn's father said, "if it's all right	67
with everyone's parents."	70
"That's a wonderful idea," Billy replied. "Thank you, Mr. Potter!"	80
While Shawn's father went to get his minivan, the other team	91
members asked their parents for permission to go to the pizza party.	103
Billy, Krista, and Jordan, who all lived nearby, got a ride with	115
Mr. Potter. Some of the other players, who lived further away,	126
planned to come with their parents.	132
On the way home, Mr. Potter stopped and picked up two pizzas.	144
Nick and Rick arrived at Shawn's house with their father, who was	156
carrying two extra-large pizzas. Soon afterward, the car pool from	167
Jefferson Street arrived. Alex, Manny, and Nicole each carried a	177
large, flat box in their hands. The aroma was unmistakable—	187
pepperoni pizza.	189
"What's happening here?" Shawn's father asked, amazed at	197
the stack of pizzas piling up.	203
Billy, Shawn, and their friends couldn't believe three sets of	213
pizzas had been ordered. "We could never eat this much pizza,"	224
they laughed.	226

© Harcourt

FLUENCY SCORE

Total Words Read Per Minute   _____

Number of Errors   − _____

Number of Words Read Correctly (WCPM) _____

Oral Reading Passage

Jake groaned when his father asked him to do the dishes. Of all his household chores, this was the one Jake disliked the most. Every time he washed the dishes, some disaster happened.

Jake sighed, walked to the kitchen, and began to run hot water in the sink. He didn't notice that a spoon was lying in the sink, just under the faucet. Immediately, water splashed off of the spoon and splattered all over the walls. Jake just grimaced and continued.

Then Jake began to squirt dishwashing liquid into the pan, but the bottle slipped in his wet hands. Dishwashing liquid oozed out, leaving a sticky stream on the window over the sink. Another sigh left Jake's throat.

Jake went on, reaching for a stack of dinner plates sitting on the counter. As he reached, his shirtsleeve caught on the handle of a skillet. The skillet shifted, bumping into some saucepans and lids. The pans and lids crashed to the floor, making a tremendous clatter. Little splatters of food from the pans lay all over the floor.

At that moment, Jake's father, hearing the noise, ran to the kitchen door. When he saw the helpless expression on Jake's face, he broke into laughter.

Oral Reading Fluency Recording Form

Name _____ Date _____

Passage 6A2   Word Count: 203

Jake groaned when his father asked him to do the	10
dishes. Of all his household chores, this was the one Jake	21
disliked the most. Every time he washed the dishes, some	31
disaster happened.	33
Jake sighed, walked to the kitchen, and began to run	43
hot water in the sink. He didn't notice that a spoon was lying	56
in the sink, just under the faucet. Immediately, water	65
splashed off of the spoon and splattered all over the walls.	76
Jake just grimaced and continued.	81
Then Jake began to squirt dishwashing liquid into the	90
pan, but the bottle slipped in his wet hands. Dishwashing	100
liquid oozed out, leaving a sticky stream on the window	110
over the sink. Another sigh left Jake's throat.	118
Jake went on, reaching for a stack of dinner plates	128
sitting on the counter. As he reached, his shirtsleeve caught	138
on the handle of a skillet. The skillet shifted, bumping into	149
some saucepans and lids. The pans and lids crashed to the	160
floor, making a tremendous clatter. Little splatters of food	169
from the pans lay all over the floor.	177
At that moment, Jake's father, hearing the noise, ran	186
to the kitchen door. When he saw the helpless expression on	197
Jake's face, he broke into laughter.	203

© Harcourt

FLUENCY SCORE

Total Words Read Per Minute   _____

Number of Errors   − _____

Number of Words Read Correctly (WCPM)   _____

Oral Reading Passage

Ferris wheels are fun rides used at carnivals, fairs, and amusement parks. Many people prefer them to roller coasters and other thrill rides because they are not as scary. Ferris wheels move slower than most roller coasters. Although Ferris wheels stand very high, they travel only in a circle. Roller coasters have drops, curves, and inclines that make them scarier. Both roller coasters and Ferris wheels rise high above the rest of the amusement park.

Most Ferris wheels stand 40 to 50 feet high and usually carry 50 to 100 people. Some roller coasters can carry more than 100 people, but most do not.

At the World's Columbian Exposition in Chicago in 1893, G. W. Gale Ferris, a mechanical engineer, built the largest of all Ferris wheels. The wheel was 250 feet in diameter. It had 36 cars that carried a total of 2,160 people. This huge Ferris wheel was used again in 1904 at the St. Louis exposition and then was sold for scrap metal.

Some people think that due to their height Ferris wheels might tip over, but there have been few accidents involving them. The wheels can withstand winds of 60 miles per hour. They may not be as exciting as roller coasters, but they appeal to those who want a more relaxing ride, and they offer riders a wonderful view.

Oral Reading Fluency Recording Form

Name _____ Date _____

Passage 6B1   Word Count: 224

Ferris wheels are fun rides used at carnivals, fairs, and amusement	11
parks. Many people prefer them to roller coasters and other thrill rides	23
because they are not as scary. Ferris wheels move slower than most roller	36
coasters. Although Ferris wheels stand very high, they travel only in a	48
circle. Roller coasters have drops, curves, and inclines that make them	59
scarier. Both roller coasters and Ferris wheels rise high above the rest of	72
the amusement park.	75
Most Ferris wheels stand 40 to 50 feet high and usually carry 50 to 100	90
people. Some roller coasters can carry more than 100 people, but most do	103
not.	104
At the World's Columbian Exposition in Chicago in 1893, G. W. Gale	116
Ferris, a mechanical engineer, built the largest of all Ferris wheels. The	128
wheel was 250 feet in diameter. It had 36 cars that carried a total of 2,160	144
people. This huge Ferris wheel was used again in 1904 at the St. Louis	158
exposition and then was sold for scrap metal.	166
Some people think that due to their height Ferris wheels might tip	178
over, but there have been few accidents involving them. The wheels can	190
withstand winds of 60 miles per hour. They may not be as exciting as	204
roller coasters, but they appeal to those who want a more relaxing ride,	217
and they offer riders a wonderful view.	224

© Harcourt

FLUENCY SCORE

Total Words Read Per Minute   _____

Number of Errors   −   _____

Number of Words Read Correctly (WCPM)   _____

Assessments for Grades 4–6

Oral Reading Passage

The great hall in the castle was the center of castle life. The lord of the castle shared living space in the great hall with most members of the household. The business of the estate was conducted in the great hall, and it was here that the men, women, and children slept. This was also the place where everyone ate together.

The lord and the lady of the castle slept at one end of the hall that was curtained off from the rest of the castle household. Lesser members of the household slept on benches along the castle walls, on straw-filled pallets, or simply on a carpet of rushes and herbs on the floor. These rushes, or grass-like plants, were frequently replaced, because they would get dirty from the grease and spillage from the food eaten in the hall.

Inside the castle, drafts of air were quite a problem because of the construction methods of the day. Proper chimneys were unknown until the late thirteenth century, and flues were often cut right through the castle walls to allow smoke to escape. It wasn't until well into the thirteenth century that carpets and tapestries made their appearance inside castles. These luxuries decorated the floors and walls, fought drafts, and improved life.

Oral Reading Fluency Recording Form

Name _____ Date _____

Passage 6B2   Word Count: 212

The great hall in the castle was the center of castle life. The	13
lord of the castle shared living space in the great hall with most	26
members of the household. The business of the estate was	36
conducted in the great hall, and it was here that the men, women,	49
and children slept. This was also the place where everyone ate	60
together.	61
The lord and the lady of the castle slept at one end of the	75
hall that was curtained off from the rest of the castle household.	87
Lesser members of the household slept on benches along the castle	98
walls, on straw-filled pallets, or simply on a carpet of rushes and	111
herbs on the floor. These rushes, or grass-like plants, were	122
frequently replaced, because they would get dirty from the grease	132
and spillage from the food eaten in the hall.	141
Inside the castle, drafts of air were quite a problem because of the	154
construction methods of the day. Proper chimneys were unknown until	164
the late thirteenth century, and flues were often cut right through the castle	177
walls to allow smoke to escape. It wasn't until well into the thirteenth	190
century that carpets and tapestries made their appearance inside castles.	200
These luxuries decorated the floors and walls, fought drafts, and improved	211
life.	212

© Harcourt

FLUENCY SCORE

Total Words Read Per Minute   _____
Number of Errors   − _____
Number of Words Read Correctly (WCPM) _____

Oral Reading Passage

Shoes are an important part of people's clothing. There are many interesting styles that people wear to be fashionable. Most shoes are made of leather, but canvas, velvet, and plastic are also used. The style of shoe people wear depends on use, custom, climate, and personal preference.

The first foot coverings were baglike wrappings made of animal fur and used in cold climates. The ancient Egyptians wore sandals made of plants and leather as early as 3700 B.C., and the Chinese began to wear wooden shoes and cloth shoes at about the same time.

Today, as well as throughout history, shoe styles come into and go out of fashion. There are casual and dress shoes for almost any occasion.

Casual shoes, usually with low heels, include the loafer, the pump, and the moccasin. These shoes are easily slipped on and have no laces or tongues. Dress shoes for women are based on the pump or sandal style and usually have a medium or high heel. Men's dress shoes are pumps made of shiny leather or Oxfords, which lace on top over a tongue.

There are tennis shoes, football shoes with rubber cleats, shoes with cushioned soles for those who walk a lot, and shoes with steel toes for protection. The desire to be fashionable and comfortable has produced many unusual kinds of shoes.

Oral Reading Fluency Recording Form

Name _____ **Date** _____

Passage 6C1   Word Count: 223

Shoes are an important part of people's clothing. There are many	11
interesting styles that people wear to be fashionable. Most shoes are made	23
of leather, but canvas, velvet, and plastic are also used. The style of shoe	37
people wear depends on use, custom, climate, and personal preference.	47
The first foot coverings were baglike wrappings made of animal fur	58
and used in cold climates. The ancient Egyptians wore sandals made of	70
plants and leather as early as 3700 B.C., and the Chinese began to wear	84
wooden shoes and cloth shoes at about the same time.	94
Today, as well as throughout history, shoe styles come into and go out	107
of fashion. There are casual and dress shoes for almost any occasion.	119
Casual shoes, usually with low heels, include the loafer, the pump,	130
and the moccasin. These shoes are easily slipped on and have no laces or	144
tongues. Dress shoes for women are based on the pump or sandal style	157
and usually have a medium or high heel. Men's dress shoes are pumps	170
made of shiny leather or Oxfords, which lace on top over a tongue.	183
There are tennis shoes, football shoes with rubber cleats, shoes with	194
cushioned soles for those who walk a lot, and shoes with steel toes for	208
protection. The desire to be fashionable and comfortable has produced	218
many unusual kinds of shoes.	223

© Harcourt

FLUENCY SCORE

Total Words Read Per Minute   _____

Number of Errors   −   _____

Number of Words Read Correctly (WCPM)   _____

Oral Reading Passage

That tall, brown mound rising from the African savannah looks like a tree stump, but it isn't. It's a termite mound, home to millions of tiny termites. Sometimes a termite mound can be as much as twenty feet high and can look like a huge sand castle.

The termites build the mound themselves. They mix the soil with their saliva to make a sticky glue, which they use to build the walls of the mound. The hot African sun bakes the walls until they are hard.

The inside of the termite mound is filled with tunnels. Tunnels let in air to cool the termites and to help them breathe. The mound also contains rooms, some of which become storerooms for food. Other rooms are nurseries in which young termites hatch and grow.

What happens when the termite eggs hatch in that maze of tunnels and rooms? Some larvae become workers, who do all the work in the mound. Others become soldiers, whose only job is to defend the termite colony. Still others become new kings and queens, who leave their "home" mound. On delicate wings they fly away to found new colonies, and soon other termite mounds rise on the savannah.

Oral Reading Fluency Recording Form

Name _____ Date _____

Passage 6C2   Word Count: 201

That tall, brown mound rising from the African savannah	**9**
looks like a tree stump, but it isn't. It's a termite mound, home to	**23**
millions of tiny termites. Sometimes a termite mound can be as	**34**
much as twenty feet high and can look like a huge sand castle.	**47**
The termites build the mound themselves. They mix the soil	**57**
with their saliva to make a sticky glue, which they use to build the	**71**
walls of the mound. The hot African sun bakes the walls until they	**84**
are hard.	**86**
The inside of the termite mound is filled with tunnels. Tunnels	**97**
let in air to cool the termites and to help them breathe. The mound	**111**
also contains rooms, some of which become storerooms for food.	**121**
Other rooms are nurseries in which young termites hatch and grow.	**132**
What happens when the termite eggs hatch in that maze of	**143**
tunnels and rooms? Some larvae become workers, who do all the	**154**
work in the mound. Others become soldiers, whose only job is to	**166**
defend the termite colony. Still others become new kings and	**176**
queens, who leave their "home" mound. On delicate wings they fly	**187**
away to found new colonies, and soon other termite mounds rise	**198**
on the savannah.	**201**

© Harcourt

FLUENCY SCORE

Total Words Read Per Minute   _____

Number of Errors   —   _____

Number of Words Read Correctly (WCPM)   _____